For the

Love

of

God

An Introduction to God

For the
Love
of
God

An Introduction to God

Liane Rich

The information contained in this book is not intended as a substitute for professional advice. Neither the publisher nor the author is engaged in rendering professional advice to the reader. The intent of the author is only to offer information of a general nature to assist you in your quest for emotional and spiritual well-being. In the event you use any of the information in this book for yourself, the author and the publisher assume no responsibility for your actions.

Loving Light Books: www.lovinglightbooks.com
Also Available at:
Amazon: www.amazon.com
Barnes & Noble: www.barnesandnoble.com

for Janie

"Is it theoretically possible to receive information from a God process, since the universal God process is inside everything?"

Gary Schwartz, Ph.D. – The G.O.D. Experiments

Preface

What would you do if you heard a very loud voice telling you that it was God and that it wanted your help to write a book? That's pretty much how it started for me about 25 years ago.

For those of you who are new to God's books and curious to know more about the source of this information, I have published this small book. It will give you a great deal of insight into the voice that speaks to me and writes through me.

For the Love of God: An Introduction to God also appears as the Introduction to our book titled, *The Book of Love.* Either book will give you greater insight into this voice and the source of this information. I thought it might be helpful to publish this introduction separately and make it available to those who might want a small "sample" before purchasing our books.

In the back of this book you will find a brief description of my first encounter with the God voice as well as a full list of book titles. I am told that repetition is used as a teaching tool in these books. God uses repetition freely and says that's the fastest way to get through our judgmental, conscious mind to the subconscious. I hand write (channel) each book and type them myself. There is no editing of this material, so you are reading the original version as it was channeled by me.

This voice originally introduced itself to me as God and I allow it to continue to share information under that name. After all these years I have come to trust and love this voice of God that speaks to me.

In Loving Light, *Liane*

For the Love of God
~ An Introduction to God ~

Now is the time I have waited for. Now is the time that I am being allowed to speak and to set the record straight. I do not wish to become repetitive in asking you to listen but it seems that repetitive asking is what is required to get you to listen.

Okay, here we go. First off, I am God and I do not hate anyone for anything they have done. Second, I do not believe it is necessary to punish in any way whatsoever. Punishment is man's creation and has nothing to do with God. Third, I do not wish to go down in history as an ogre. I do not condemn anyone to hellfire for eternity and I will never take part in such actions. If you wish to teach that God is a punishing ruler, I wish you to stipulate that it is your belief that such a God exists, but that your belief has no relationship to the truth.

If I could speak I would tell you to please stop fighting and to please begin to love one another. You do not seem to love yourself and you do not seem to know how to love. In this book (this is a reference to *The Book of Love*) I will try to explain how you have become so disconnected from love. I speak now of true, unconditional, all accepting love. This is the love that is of God. God does not make rules for you to live by and then punish you for not following these rules. I am love. I am not darkness and anger and vengeance. I do not punish and I do not wish anyone to believe that I would be so unfair as to wipe out entire worlds due to a decision that said worlds were sinners.

God does not believe in sin. God *does* believe in love, acceptance, peace, enlightenment, trust and faith, and even joy. Stop teaching that I believe in death and destruction for those who do not follow the rules. I am God and I have *no* rules and I will not harm anyone. I am not a harmful, nor a punishing, nor a vengeful God. Please stop believing such things about me. Do not allow yourself to be convinced that God is not all-loving, all-caring, and all-accepting. I do not create my children so that I might punish them. There are many ways to teach a child without the need for punishment.

I do not wish you to continue to believe in hell and damnation. Let it all go! God does not round you up after death and herd you into some fiery pit if you have sinned. This is not what I do. Do you see how you have made me into a villain?

How can you possibly love me without fear if you only see me as a judge? I am not a judge. I am not an ogre. I am not a villain, and I certainly do not wish you harm in any way.

You will find that I am quite loving and very kind. The kindness of God is boundless. When you meet someone who is showing you kindness you will know that they are from God. I am trying to express through matter at this time and it is most difficult. If God could speak would you listen? If I were to tell you that I can sometimes break through the barrier that exists between us to communicate my message to you, would you listen? Will you believe me? If I ask you to stop all this nonsense about war and fighting will you listen? If I tell you that I am God and I'm trying to get through to you to save you from your own destruction, will you listen?

Will you accept that God doesn't fight, that God doesn't war in heaven with angels of the devil or dark forces? Will you believe me? Can you exist in peace with one another and with God, or do you require some form of antagonism in order to feel secure in all that you are? Are you able to allow God to be all-loving and unconditional in that love? Will you allow God to be God instead of someone man has created out of his *need* for penance?

Yes, man created his belief in a vengeful,

judgmental God who is all powerful and aggressive in order to fill a need for restriction. Man is so afraid of his own nature that he has created this great controlling, dominating figure to watch over and control him. Why? Because man has great fear regarding his own creative nature and even his destructive nature. So what does he do? He creates a belief in an all-knowing, all-punishing, and once in a while rewarding, authority figure. Do not pin this personality, which you have created to fulfill your own needs, on me. I am not that narrow and small and limited. I am totally unlimited in my light and awareness. When one is totally unlimited one does not react nor does one enjoy acting such a role as judge.

Let go of everything you think you know. I am God and I am here to speak out to anyone who is ready to hear. I do not judge. I do not live in your world of cruelty and I do not expect you to be any way other than what you are. I am the creator and you are the creation. I will tell you who and what you are and I do not expect you to say who or what I am. I am love. Very simply put, I am the love and the light of the world and I am trying to get through the darkness and fear that surrounds you so that I might tell you I love you unconditionally – no strings attached – no rules attached. Just God loving and accepting and watching over his creation with kindness and gentleness.

You get to *choose* what you believe in, you know? You can believe in a God who is going to love and accept you no matter what, or you can believe in a God who wishes to control your behavior. You choose.

༺࿇༻

As you begin to understand the truth about God you will see how you have been told untruths and even how you have been led to believe that God is not as he truly *is*. God is born of light and love and I will not have a few who do not understand begin to unravel the good I have created. If you continue to teach that God is creating chaos and ending worlds to bring everything into balance you are sadly mistaken. God does not create so that he might destroy. Most of what God creates is from love and some is from curiosity. Never did I create out of a need to punish. I did not run anyone out of Eden and I do not care what fruit anybody eats. I don't even care if you sin. Sin is your way of acting out and I do not care if you act out or not.

You may begin to see how I am not what you have always believed by looking at why you believe me to be a punishing God. Who told you that I send bad people or children (as you are <u>all</u> my children) to hell? Who told you I would wipe out civilizations for their sins and wrongdoing? Why do you believe it and where does it come from? I believe you will find that such stories of a punishing type God are handed down from generation to generation. I believe you will also see that you are taught to not question what you are learning in regards to these traditional beliefs. You were taught to accept and to believe in this punishing God. If you do not believe in this big control freak you are taught that you will be separated and chastised and not saved. And why would you believe it's important to be saved? Because the ones teaching about this big controlling God are teaching that he is so controlling that he cannot accept *any* who do not see things his way.

I am not this God! How can I convince you that you are being taught and trained to fear a God that does not exist? I must wait for you to return in death and by then the damage is done and the "fear of God" is in place. Do not fear God and please – I beg of you – do not put the fear of God in others.

Some of you are motivated by fear and so you use fear to motivate others. I wish this pattern, or trend, to stop. Stop trying to control others by teaching them that they will perish in hell if they do not believe as you believe. Allow the others to live as they see fit and do not tell them your lies about God. God does not wish his children to be subjected to the rules certain groups and organizations have set in place out of their need for a controlling, punishing, authority figure. I will not play that role for you and you may wait until eternity for this god of yours to punish you and send you off to hell, but it will *never* happen. This I promise you! I wish to clear up a few things in this book (this is a reference to *The Book of Love*) and I wish you to use your infinite wisdom to return to love and leave fear behind.

≈❧≈

*W*hen you begin to understand that it is not man who created God but rather God who created man, you will realize that it is not your place to call God an authority figure. God is no such figure. In fact, God is rather energy. You will not find God sporting robes and long hair. You will not find God floating on clouds and spouting sermons. You will, however, see how God is bright light energy.

God is the love energy that is alive and well in everyone and everything. God does not sit on his golden throne and watch over his people. This is a God created out of man's imagination and man's need to have something or someone higher in power and position than himself.

If you could do one thing to please God, you would be allowing God to control over you. You submit to God what is God's in an effort to have a supreme parent. I am not a supreme parent and I do not rule over my children like a judge rules over his county. I am God. I am a gentle pulsating light energy and I do not wish to be seen as a holy, insensitive power head. I wish to be seen as energy.

Now, herein lies the problem. You, as humans, do not know how to love, respect and appreciate energy. If I say that I am God and I look like man or have a personality that resembles that of humans, you can understand and relate to me. When you take away my human traits and make me into a vibrating light, you do not know how to embrace and hug a light. This is our biggest problem. If I tear away the curtain of myth, how might you love me? If I no longer have the appeal of being human-like and having personality, how can you relate to me? If I let go of the image you have projected on me, how can you still relate to something beyond yourself? Personal relationship

16

with "light" is quite difficult for you at this time. I know that you do not actually think of me as a man but you also do not think of me as I truly am.

So, what shall God do? Do I leave you with your image intact and continue to allow you to project new harmful pain and judgment because of that image, or do I tell you how it truly is and risk losing contact with you altogether? It is most difficult to make these assessments and to know how you will eventually respond in the future. You have proven to be quite strong in your beliefs and quite needy in certain areas concerning right and wrong and rules. How will I get you to drop your rules and allow everything to simply be? I think I will allow you to see me any way you please....

This will allow me to be seen by you in the way that you most need me. If you need someone to tell you how wrong or bad you are, you may project that onto me as you have in the past. On the other hand, if you want to raise your level of consciousness you may begin by seeing me as light. I am the light and I am the way you return to light. Energy is not bad or good. Energy emits light and allows all to occur. You are returning to the light and you are beginning to see things from a new perspective. If you return to the light, you will then know my true identity and this game of unconsciousness will end. If you choose not to return, you will continue to play this game.

It is a win/win situation. Those who continue to believe in a nonjudgmental, all-accepting, loving God will continue to move toward the light. Those who continue to believe in a judging, condemning God will be allowed to continue to play the game and stay unconscious. You cannot lose. It is set up so that no one is *wrong*. Everyone simply makes a choice and moves in the direction of said choice. Think of it as a journey or vacation. You get to go whichever direction you choose. No one loses, no one is wrong. Everyone has simply made a choice and is moving toward the choice they have made.

This is the biggest reason for allowing everyone to believe exactly what they believe. Each are going on a trip and this trip was planned by their soul before they even entered a body.

Now, you think on this for awhile while I speak with my pen (Liane) on a personal matter.

❧

As you begin to see God in a whole new way, you may begin to lose your fear of God. This is my hope. God is feared to the extent that it is impossible for you to embrace him. Many have switched their attention over to my one and only begotten son, Jesus the Christ. Jesus is not my one and only begotten son, as you are all sons and daughters and plants and trees and rocks and oceans of God. I created you all and I sent you all into matter. I basically projected my energy outward and entered matter. This was done gradually as it is difficult for pure light energy to become solid.

After you *became* human, you began to find ways in which you could contact me. One of these was through intuitive ability and another was through *idea* or *thought*. You might say that you thought God into your material world in an effort to stay connected. Now you think of God when you need help or assistance and this too is good.

So, here you are entering the material plane and you wish to stay connected. You began to experiment *in* matter and to use your God-given creative abilities. This began a process by which you began to fear and judge what you created. Not always, but often you would create and say, "Oh no, this is not good enough, I must do better." This was soon followed by, "Oh no, this is awful" and then came, "Oh no, this is bad" and voilà, we now have created bad and its opposite which is good. So now we have bad and good, and we wish to continue to create so we simply allow for mistakes by saying we will deal with it later. After many, many mistakes we begin to feel bad and this creates guilt. We now have guilt and its opposite which is innocence.

So now we have you all creating and believing in bad and awful and guilt. Once guilt was in place there was a need for punishment to assuage the guilt. So now we need a big strong punishing figure and who do we project this task onto? Right! You sent this job or this energy back to God. You wanted someone or something to intervene and stop the awful creations. By the way, these creations were only awful in your eyes and were perfectly acceptable in God's eyes. So now we have you projecting the guilt and judgment back to God and God accepted all, as God is aware and enlightened and sees from a broad perspective that all is harmless and nothing is anything other than God's created glory. You send this energy back to God and expect God to play parent and punish you when you believe you have done wrong, only God does not punish. God only loves!

So what can you do about this situation? You can continue to call on God to punish and reward you for your creations or you can take that job upon yourself. Some of you do, you know? You can't wait until you die and have God as your judge to hand down the penance, so you begin to punish yourself now. You let your guilt and fear eat away at you a little at a time. Now I would like you to stop this nonsense. I am God and I will not send anyone to hell now or ever. I have never sent anyone to such a place and I never would. You may choose to make yourself miserable with the belief in a punishing God, but that is all it is. It is your belief and it is created by you, not by God.

Allow yourselves to accept God as he truly is. It is not necessary to frighten yourself with the promise of hell for your mistakes. *God does not punish*. God only rewards and loves and nurtures. How did you get it so mixed up and off base? God is love. How can love punish? Only fear punishes, love does not. If you punish someone, it is out of fear. Fear that this child or person may not learn the rules and behave properly. Fear that this person will leave you, or fear that this person might be harmed for not following your rules. You *never* punish out of love. No one punishes out of love. You might restrict a child, or restrain them from running out and harming themselves, but you do not inflict physical pain out of love. You inflict physical pain and emotional trauma out of fear, and sometimes out of your own *need* to inflict pain or injury.

Do not punish. Be as God and begin to love and accept. "Spare the rod, spoil the child" is not a good idea and has consequences created by the act itself. Each time you strike someone, be it a child or an adult, it results in energy that will evolve into something else. Everything is energy in movement and when you strike out to hurt someone, energy moves within you and that energy says, "It is okay to hit and it is okay to hurt." So now you have a belief *in* hitting and hurting and this will become your reality. You will now live in a world of hitting and hurting.

So, keep your world pain free and punishment free. Do not strike out at anyone and do not call upon God to strike out at others, because it all comes back to you, as you are the creator of your own reality and you do not affect others as much as you affect yourself. God will not strike out for you and God does not require you to create this reality for him. God is love and will continue to be love. No heaven, no hell, just God constantly watching over creation in a very gentle, calm way, and loving and accepting all that you do.

❧

You will begin to see change in how you view God when you begin to let go of your restrictions on God. You are restricting God by allowing him to be only what you wish him to be.

In my discussions with you I must use the pronoun he or him when discussing God. This is due to the fact that so few of you believe God to be female in nature. Actually God is everything and anything you can think of. God is even *thought*. So, if God is everything you see and even don't see, how can you continue to call him by a male pronoun? This is something that will not change any time soon, so in my communications with you I continue to use the words that you can best relate to. God is actually energy and God takes up all space and time. You will find nothing that exists outside of God.

So, if nothing exists outside of God, how is it that you continue to place yourself outside of God? How is it that you do not believe yourself to be God? How is it that you think of yourself as created by God, but not part of God? How is it that you have separated yourself so completely from this God energy? How can you return to God without going through the whole dying and judgment routine? And when do you return to your true nature of God energy? These are just some of the questions I will try to answer for you in this book (this is a reference to *The Book of Love*). I would like you to know that I have written other books for you through this particular channel. This woman who writes for me leads a very quiet life and wishes to retain her privacy. I will allow her this request.

Now, when you begin to see God as more than a judge, you will see he has a nature that is continuously loving and giving. "God giveth and God taketh away" is not an exactitude. The phrase should go more like "God is constantly changing." God does not take away, however God is energy and energy moves and changes with the conditions it is exposed to. So, as God moves and changes, you begin to see changes in your life. You begin to feel changes, and by your nature, you too are energy and part of God, so you also are changing and moving with conditions.

You are partly responsible for everything that occurs in your life. You are co-creators with God and you are God energy. The God energy that is in you is so very important and most of you do not even know it is there. You are walking around with God *in* you and you don't know it. You are acting as though God is a personality who sits up in the sky and watches over you all day. You get this identity from watching families. Family situations are made up of many dynamics, one of which is that there is always someone to watch over and direct the young ones, so they do not go astray.

When you are quite small, this is more of a loving nurturing situation. You get held and hugged a lot because you are so tiny and so cute. As you age a bit, this situation becomes more of a guardian role, whereby you are watched over so you will not do wrong or make mistakes. As you become pubescent, this role of nurturing and loving pretty much reaches its limit, as you are now doing your own thing and learning to say "no" to anyone you do not agree with. By this stage of the game you have become rebellious and must be warned and threatened with punishment for breaking the rules.

By pubescence you are breaking away, leaving home and getting ready to set out on your own. This is the stage that you last experience as a child and it is most important. The child leaves home and goes out into the world to make his or her own way and you are now without your beloved little one. You want your child back. Mostly you want someone to love, so you stay as close as possible to your child in hopes they might return. This is the stage that is most powerful in the human psyche. You all come into a family. It is the only way to come to earth at this time. Therefore this is a universal experience and it is also the most powerful, because it is universal.

So, this is where your belief in a judging controlling God comes from. Originally man had an idea of the God/man connection. This idea became more of a threat, and was associated with

Liane Rich

punishment, only after thousands of years of memory association. These memories primarily said, "We come from God. We left God. God wants us back. We must be punished if we break the rules and leave for good." In the same way that a teenager is threatened with, "You won't make it on your own, you'll see. You'll come running back begging for my help and forgiveness, and I won't be there. You're on your own now. See how well you do without me." Something along these lines, but you get the idea.

So now we have everyone beginning to project this parental image onto a higher parental image, and here we have it. God sits in heaven waiting for his unruly children to return so he might give them their just desserts. And what does that mean? Be good to God or you will have hell to pay later! This is so not true! Please, please do not believe this. You do not go to a made up place called hell. You do not burn in fire and damnation for eternity. You do not displease God and you certainly do not need to fear God.

❧

*A*s you continue to see God as an authority

figure and a judge, you will continue to have fear of death. How can one believe that God would send sinners to burn for eternity for simply having a belief that is not Christian? The biggest concern here is that God will always judge. God does not judge and he never has been that human. The only part of God who judges, are the humans who have come *from* God. You who are in this human condition do not know how to live without judgment and so you see God as judging also.

Once you begin to see God as energy you will be more inclined to work with God and less inclined to simply obey God. God is not a ruler with rules. I do not make rules for you to live by and follow. You as humans require and request rules. You believe that without the rules you would not be safe from yourself and from others. You have set the rules by which you might live, because you fear retaliation and punishment. You fear being punished by God, or the gods, and so you created rules to keep you in line and safe. Just the thought of no rules terrifies you. You would no longer have rules to enforce and everyone would do whatever they felt like doing with no repercussions.

So, rules work for you. You need rules to keep you safe from fear and you need rules to keep you in line. Now it is time to let go of some of these rules. You are going to be brave and face your fears and realize that God does not punish. God does not reward. God simply *is*. God is love and God is light. God is everything and God is nothing.

God is what you make him to be. For now you are making him out to be a judge. Let go of this image of God and start with a whole new image. See God as energy that lives *inside* of you, that flows through you and is part of your makeup. Start to see God as love and light emanating from you. Go out into the world each day and be aware that God is in you and with you. Walk with God within you and act as though you know it. Act as though you are carrying the most precious gift right inside of you. *Act as though God is part of you and therefore you are part of God.* Act as though you are with God in all that you do. See God as energy – light energy – running through your body and affecting your entire day. Walk through life as though you have a partner in life. This partner is God and God is always *in* you and *with* you and part of you.

⁓

You will become God by knowing that you are one with God. You do not become God by worshiping God and pretending that God is separate from you.

You all have creative force running through you, and this creative force is God force. God is energy. This energy that is God takes up all space and all time. You are not outside of this energy and you are definitely not separate from this energy. You react with it and you live *in* it. You live *in* God and you react with God every minute of every day.

To realize the extent to which you are connected to God, you must first see how it is impossible for you to be separate or away from God. God is *in* you and God is *outside* of you. God is in the air that you breathe and the sky that you see. God is in nature and God is in water and God is in plants and everything you eat and drink. God is the energy that holds the particles together. God is the glue that holds the world together. God is the string of energy that connects absolutely everything. *Everything* is God!

Now, I realize that this idea may not sit well with you who believe in Satan and evil, but this is how it is. This is the truth and to let go of your belief in evil would be a wise choice. You see, there really is no evil. There is only misperception, mistranslation and distortion of what is. God does not create devils and evil doers. Man creates these out of his need for punishment and rules. Man believes he will go astray if he is not kept in line. He somehow has come to the conclusion that certain parts of his nature are dangerous, and therefore undesirable and even evil. Man has come to see evil inside himself as well as others. Man has created evil in order to punish himself for doing anything that he considers out of line. The evil factor is used to describe the devil and bad people.

So, here is my question to you. If God takes up all time and all space, how does evil fit into God? "Evil is separate from God," you say. No, evil is not separate. Everything in creation is of God. It came from God and it still is God. You do not go forth from your creator and suddenly disconnect from that creator. You may move forward into creation but what are you? You are the energy of the creator. You are God projected into creation. You are what you came from, and what you came from is God.

༄༅

Once you begin to see God as part of yourself, you will be allowed to love yourself. If you know that you are carrying God *within* you, you will be less likely to hate you. Your problems on earth now come from low self-esteem and even self-loathing. If you believe strongly that God is riding inside of everyone, you will be kinder and more loving toward everyone.

You are at the point in your evolution that is most critical. You are at the point of self-destruction and I wish you to know that you cannot destroy God. God rides in you and God surrounds you. You can't get *out* of God and you can't get away from God. You can only become more aware of God or less aware of God. *In teaching that God is above you and outside of you, you are teaching separation from God.* You do not wish to be separate from God, and so I am communicating with you now in order to assist you in *shifting* your awareness of God. This will allow you to reconnect with God, which in turn will allow you to love yourself once again.

So, God is within you and God is within your neighbor. This is the part you don't like. You love the idea that God may be within you and ready to assist you, but you do not like the idea that God is also in everyone else. This means you must treat everyone with a great deal of respect. Respect comes hard for you as you do not respect you, so how can you possibly respect others? You are so afraid of being low man out that you constantly compete and struggle to be the best. You are all programmed to be the best and, when you are expected to be the best, someone is made into the worst. It is the law of polarities. To have "best" you must then create "worst." To have "good" you must then create "bad," and to have "God" you then create God's opposite which you call the devil or evil. No such thing exists and no one ever sees the devil or Satan at death. This is simply a game you play with yourself so you can stay good and do your best!

You do not need to be the best at anything. Competition thrives on earth at this time because you are all trying to outdo one another. Let go of this *need* to be 'better than' and begin to see how 'being respectful' is your number one goal. This is the assignment I would like to give you today. Go out into the world and show respect for everyone you meet. Anyone who crosses your path is carrying God inside, so please show them respect and kindness. Do not be so sure that the idiots you have labeled as too stupid are really all that stupid. Some souls come to show you who you are and how you can evolve.

෧෴෫

You will begin to see how God is energy and how God is in you by allowing yourself to calm down and be at peace. Part of the reason for believing that God is not part of you is that you constantly move and shake and distort your emotional body. Your emotional body is at such a stress level that I may never get through to you. You are constantly stressed over a situation or depressed about your life. If not depressed or stressed, you are in a state of denial regarding events in your life, and some of you are so worried about your place in life, that you cannot hear or feel God. I want you to hear me and I want you to *feel* me. This may take some doing but we will come to a place that is most conducive for God and man to merge. God will know man, and man will know God.

As far as God is concerned it does not really matter that you believe he is not present *in* you. One of these days God will show himself to you and you will have a new perspective on who and what God is. For now I wish you to know that I am *in* you and you are part of me.

So, if God is in you and you are part of God, how is it that you are so unconscious of this fact? You are unconscious because you are growing into what you will one day become. You are in an evolutionary phase, and you are becoming conscious at a very slow rate in order to preserve the density of matter. Once you awaken, or become conscious of the fact that you carry God *in* you, you will begin to vibrate at a much greater rate. This allows you to chip away at the hard matter that surrounds you. This allows you to break out of the mold that has encased you – sort of like a chicken who cracks his egg open and sees daylight for the very first time.

You will be cracking the code that has kept you locked in and afraid of God. You must break down your fear of a punishing God before you can accept that God is *in* you. How would it be to accept God as *in* you and to believe that this God, who is in you, is going to punish you for being bad or not being baptized or not believing in this book or that book? If God is in you and going to punish you for your beliefs or non-beliefs you are then in quite a struggle. You are in a fight over who owns you. You are in a debate over who will rule the body. If God lives in you and you hold the belief that God will send you to heaven or hell, you will constantly struggle to maintain control and diplomacy over your domain.

So, God allowed you to separate and to believe that God is separate from you. You are now in a position to break down the old barriers and begin to accept God into you. Can you do this? Can you allow God his correct place in creation? God is allowed to be a ruler up in the clouds; can you now allow God to be in you, with you, part of you?

❧

*W*hen you begin to see how you are all God energy, you will begin to become aware of your connection to God. You will see how God is running through you and you will see how God is in everything. The best way to begin to realize your God nature is to begin to understand how you are programmed. You are all programmed to be who you think you are. You are all told what you know and you are all trained from infancy to believe this or to believe that.

This type of programming is meant to raise you up into an adult. One of the reasons you use programming is simply that it works. If you teach someone something enough times, in enough different ways, it will eventually sink in. If you run with a certain group you begin to act and sound like the rest of your group. You actually program quite easily so it is not difficult to get you to imitate and follow. You see this often in fashion and technology. Everyone wants the latest trend and no one likes being left out. You are very easily trained to follow and some are easily trained to become leaders. Others, in armies, are subjected to circumstances in which they become susceptible to choices they would not naturally make. One can be programmed strongly enough to become a killing machine.

So, if you can be so easily programmed, can you also be un-programmed or change your programming? Yes! The answer to this is yes. I am here now in the hopes of feeding you enough of the truth, that you will let go of the lies you have been taught and told over and over. This is no easy task, as your programming is quite strong and has been in place for a very long time.

Your programming began at a time when you were less sophisticated in your thinking. Most of mankind developed a belief in a punishing God the first time a storm rolled in. No one could imagine any other reason back then. It could only be that someone had inadvertently displeased the gods. This led to a belief in injustice, and of course its opposite which is justice. This led to punishment for any infraction or injustice, and this led to finding others and yourself guilty. We now have guilt, punishment and justice all related to God. It all started simply enough, with a very simple-minded and superstitious time in your history. Now you are a little more evolved and God is still getting a bad rap.

It is not God who storms overhead and destroys your crops. It is not God who creates floods to wipe out entire cities. It is not God's will that you be punished or suffer in any way. It is not God's will to strike you down for your sins. Everything is simply a state of growth, and growth means change. A baby grows into an adult and you no longer have a cute cuddly little bundle to coo at you. You now have a rather large person who may from time to time yell loudly and demand things. This is not God punishing you, this is growth and it is life in material form. Life in material form will always move and grow because it is life. It is energy moving and growing and vibrating and changing. Growth is simply part of evolution, and it has little to do with your personal preference of wanting everything to stay nice and small and cuddly and cute.

Life grows and life changes. Life is meant to move. When life moves in a direction that frightens you, you tend to blame God. When life moves in a direction you consider good, you tend to thank God. It is all the same. I do not take away and I do not give. I am simply the creator of all creation. I watch, I love, I accept, I adore and I am. I do not rob you to give to someone else, and I do not change or manipulate the energy so that you can be saved. You do this. You are the one who makes the choices. You are the one who responds and you are the one who creates in your current situation.

You create it all. You ask for it and you complain about it. You create by your need and your belief. You are programmed to believe certain things, and these beliefs send out strong thought energy which circles around you and creates your reality for you. Please watch your thoughts and beliefs. You come from God and God is creative energy. You carry God in you. You carry creative energy in you. You are creating with this creative force that you carry. You are projecting energy outward and creating for yourself. Allow only the best, most positive to go forward from you. Allow love to be your predominant goal and you will be creating from love. Do not blame God for the next upset in your life. Look into yourself and see how you have sent out energy to change your situation. Then begin to look at how this change may possibly be a gift. So often you hate big change and yet in the end it is a great gift.

I do not expect you to see God and creation differently overnight. I am planting seeds and beginning to program you in a whole new way. Welcome to God's world and God's perspective. Sit back and enjoy as I begin to share some truth, which is light awareness, with you....

(See *The Book of Love* to continue reading.)

Introduction to
The Loving Light Books Series

There are many ways to go within to your core or your heart center. When you reach deep within your own psyche you will enter the core of your being. This is where soul and spirit resides.

For those of you who wish to reconnect with your own God-self I highly suggest that you read and reread the "Loving Light Books" series. This series is designed to draw you "within" to your own God-self and to allow you to peel away the layers that prevent you from becoming the loving, radiant being that you truly are.

This series of books was received by my pen (Liane) over a 10 year span of time and are quite remarkable. You will be led from an earthly way of viewing life to a more God-like way of viewing life. Everything is subjective in this three-dimensional world that you now call home. You, however, are a spiritual being and your life as a human is out of balance since you decided to enter matter. We will feed you information in this series that will allow you to *perceive* your current life in a whole new way.

These books were written for my channel and are most helpful to anyone who wishes to add more love and understanding to their life here on earth. If you are happy with where your life stands now, I do wish you well. If, on the other hand, you would like to learn more about your own spirit essence and how to connect with the part of you that draws love and unconditional light into your life, I highly suggest you begin your journey *within* by reading these helpful books.

I wish you well on your journey to discovering "you"....

God

The Loving Light Books Series

Book 1: God Spoke through Me to Tell You to Speak to Him
Book 2 & 3: No One Will Listen to God & You are God
Book 4: The Sun and Beyond
Book 5: The Neverending Love of God
Book 6: The Survival of Love
Book 7: We All Go Together
Book 8: God's Imagination
Book 9: Forever God
Book 10: See the Light
Book 11: Your Life as God
Book 12: God Lives
Book 13: The Realization of Creation
Book 14: Illumination
Book 15: I Touched God
Book 16: I and God are One
Book 17: We All Walk Together
Book 18: Love Conquers All
Book 19: Come to the Light of Love
Book 20: The Grace is Ours

Also by Liane Rich

The Book of Love
For the Love of God: An Introduction to God
For the Love of Money: Creating Your Personal Reality
Your Individual Divinity: Existing in Parallel Realities
For the Love of Life on Earth
Your Return to the Light of Love: a guidebook to spiritual awakening

God's Pen

I first heard the voice of God in 1988. I was sitting in my back yard reading a book when this big booming voice interrupted with, "I am God and I will not come to you by any other name." I felt like the voice was everywhere – inside of me as well as in the sky around me. I was so frightened that I ran in my bedroom to hide.

This was not the first time that I heard voices. I had been communicating with my own spirit guide or soul for about a year. I guess my depth of fear regarding God, and all that he represented to me at the time, was just too much.

I spent two days trying to avoid the voice of God, which was patiently waiting for me to respond. By the second day I was exhausted from lack of sleep and decided to give in and talk with him. This turned out to be the greatest gift and best decision of my life.

In the beginning the voice of God would wake me in the middle of the night and tell me it was time to write. He said I had promised to do this work (I assumed he was talking about the soul/spirit me). I would drag myself up to a sitting position and watch in amazement as my hand flew across the page, while I tried to keep up by reading what was being written.

It was always so much fun to wake up the

next morning and grab my notebook to see what God had written during the night. After some time the voice stopped waking me and I became comfortable picking up my pen and writing for God first thing in the morning. I think in the beginning I had to be awakened while still semi-conscious from sleep so I wouldn't object too much to the information that was being channeled through me.

As I grew less and less afraid (and more trusting) of God, he was able to communicate greater information. Some of the information is quit controversial, but I felt it important to just let it be and not censor it. I present the writings in this book to you as they were given to me.

For privacy reasons I am using a pen name. I asked God for a good pen name and he guided me to Liane which (I was told) in Hebrew means "God has answered."

At one point I became a little concerned about my sanity in all this, so I went to a hypnotherapist to find out what I was doing. Under hypnosis I saw this incredibly huge beam of light with a voice coming from within it. It was a giant "loving light" and felt so comforting and kind. It felt like that's where I came from. After that I stopped worrying about my sanity. If this is crazy, I think it's a very good kind of crazy to be....

In loving light, Liane

Loving Light Books

Available at:
Loving Light Books: www.lovinglightbooks.com
Amazon: www.amazon.com
Barnes & Noble: www.barnesandnoble.com

Also on Request at Local Bookstores

www.ingramcontent.com/pod-product-compliance
Lightning Source LLC
Chambersburg PA
CBHW030308030426
42337CB00012B/635